Sibling Rivalry Press, LLC
PO Box 26147
Little Rock, AR 72221

info@siblingrivalrypress.com

www.siblingrivalrypress.com

ISBN: 978-1-943977-79-6

By special invitation, this title is housed in the Rare Book and Special Collections Vault of the Library of Congress.

First Sibling Rivalry Press Edition, September 2020

LESBIAN
fashion struggles

CAROLINE EARLEYWINE

SIBLING RIVALRY PRESS
DISTURB/ENRAPTURE
LITTLE ROCK, ARKANSAS

For Bonnie—you are the reason I wrote my first love poem.

And for my LGBTQ students—I have borrowed your bravery and you inspire me daily. I am who I am because of you.

TABLE OF CONTENTS

Jenny: You knew they were lesbians, right?

Mark: That's true.

Jenny: So what do you think it is?

Mark: I don't know. I'd say it has something to do with their attitude. It's not that their masculine or anything, because actually some of them are pretty feminine, you know? They have these haircuts. These very cool haircuts. Hey, don't get me wrong, it's obviously more than a haircut, that's true. It's something they exude, it's… I'm gonna try to put my finger on it.

Jenny: Good. Tell me when you do, Mark.

– The L Word –

When we speak we are afraid our words will not be heard or welcomed. But when we are silent, we are still afraid. So it is better to speak.

– Audre Lorde –

Where I Come from

I have relatives long gone, women
from the Old South who never married—
who lived in their aprons and their closets
and I think of that Mississippi

swelter, that suffocating silence
and so I say I have a girlfriend
and I say it on Thanksgiving
in the kitchen while my aunts

do the dishes and I think of my parents'
closed doors, the hushed words
behind them, how I never saw a kiss
or an *I love you* between them

and so I tell her I love how she touches
me, her gentle hands, the spell of her
kiss and I say I love her until I don't
feel so naked, or until even naked

feels safe and I say *that hurt
my feelings* even when it feels silly—
I fill the tension with words
until we scratch our way out

and I talk and I talk and I open
my mouth because they couldn't,
because they can't
anymore.

Granddaddy's Closet

So much had built up to this—
my 93-year-old grandfather across from me
and between us, this secret.

His first response was a question:
Do you think it runs in families?

He then told me about his brother
who never married, who he always
wondered about.

After he assured me he thought no differently
of me, he asked if I wanted any of his old clothes.

My grandfather was always a practical
gift giver. Made us homemade hangers
for Christmas. Gave the girl cousins kitchen sponges

and the boy cousins pocket knives.
But on this day, he brought out a box

of his cardigans and sweaters,
his flannel shirts. He laid them
out on the floor for me to look through,

to take whatever I thought
I needed.

Femme Invisibility

At the store I try
on lipstick. The pink
shade floats in the shape
of my mouth, suspended silent
in the middle of the aisle.

The waiter brings two separate
checks to the table, overlooks
our still moving forks, assumes
we dined and dashed.

At the family reunion, my dad
introduces us as *roommates, friends*,
then vaguely gestures at the place
where we once stood.

Sometimes I disappear, but
on the car ride home
you reach for my hand,
your thumb grazing across
my palm and the car fills
with light. I am so seen
I glow.

Blonde

Before I knew what it was to be scared, I braided black yarn into my long blonde hair. A dash of darkness to match my chain belt and plaid pants. To match my parents' rotting marriage, my trendy angst. I pretended it belonged there—that I had grown such a thing.

When I became pretty as a punchline boys made about dumb girls, I twirled it between my fingers. I collected moments of men running their hands through it, tangled and dirty the morning after, sighing about *how long* it was.

You're that blonde girl.
You're the prettiest I've ever
slept with. You're the most
beautiful woman I've ever seen
at the bars.

The magazines say men prefer it hanging down to the middle of my back. They don't say this makes me more of a target, that it can be fashioned into an extra limb to grab, one that can't hit back. My hair followed me to bars, extending invitations to men without consulting me.

And he'd been no different. He'd slipped drink after drink to my hair, wrapped it around his knuckles and asked it to dance, to let out a schoolgirl giggle. To sit on his lap, its strands draping across the sticky bar floor.

It was years before I learned the true story of Medusa: Poseidon, the guy at the bar circling her in a cloud of smoke, an ocean waiting to swallow her whole. Medusa blamed for her short skirt. Her long hair. For the drink in her hand, for her existence, for what he took. Instead in the stories, we name the one who beheaded her *Hero*, the one who raped her *a God*. Instead, we name her *Monster*, because what else would you call a woman with power? A woman with a gaze that's stronger than yours?

Back at the bar, my hair was wrapped around his knuckles, his body an ocean tidal-waving toward me. I never thought of cutting it before that day. Fourteen inches, two yellow thick tails that had to be bound with rubber bands. The day I left him, the day I left all of them, the twin snakes of my hair writhed on the floor. They grew fangs and I told them your names.

Lipstick

I've shied away from any shade
not camouflage, flinched when
he asked me to wear a dress or
when she prefers the old photo,
the one with my hair long. That
kind of woman seemed weak.
Soft. Less howl, more whisper.
Less take and more give. I have
been washed out and smudged,
worn down to a nub, a color so
faint it wouldn't leave a mark on
a collar or a dick or someone
else's mouth. It wouldn't tell.
Lately I dream about lipstick.
About staining my lips bright,
walking down aisles lined with
bullets of color to choose the
perfect shot. One to make my
mouth a bloody declaration.
Bright as a dare, not a blushing
apology, a shade so loud it
breaks teeth. Demands I close
my fingers around its trigger,
open my barrel of a mouth and
shoot.

A Public Dog

I heard him whistle at our girl before I saw him.
Bullet sirens, short and loud, a call meant to charm
her from the basket of her cower, make her dance
into his arms. He reached down before we could
stop him. Ignored the spiked army of fur at full
attention down her back, the ears slicked down,
the low growl, her only language for saying *No*.
Still he reached, even as her growl grew to a bark.
She lunged toward him, my wife struggling to pull
her back. He didn't move. Said over her barking,
still reaching, *Is it mean?*

Yes, don't touch her. We tugged on her leash, worked
to move us out of the space that was ours before
the man came in to claim it. He smirked. Lit a cigarette.
Stood his ground and called after us as we rushed
away, *She don't seem like a public dog.*

Why I Cut My Hair
Why I Have Tattoos
Why Most Clothes I Wear
Don't Feel like They Fit

Because there is no power
in a sheep in sheep's clothes,
no mystery without
the wolf underneath.

Because I would rather growl
and bark and scrape for every
appearance of strength than admit
to the disappointment of my bite,

to the dullness of my teeth.
Because I'll wear my wounds
like battle scars from wars I chose
to fight when really you drafted me

without so much as a word and it took
years for me to hear the echo of my
own silence, to acknowledge the clarity
and eloquence of my first *No*, to remember

the nights I can't remember.
Because I do not claim
the innocence of white fleece
or the toughness of claws,

I am a nameless creature
under all of these layers, I am
digging and digging and have yet
to hit the skin of me.

Hatshepsut

My childhood obsession. Egyptian Queen turned
Pharaoh. When her husband died, she not only took
his throne, but his clothes, insisted on being painted
with a beard. I drew a picture of her coronation day
for history class: Hatshepsut on a carrying chair

held on the backs of men, wearing facial hair
and eyeliner, everyone bowing to this rebel in
a headdress, this temple of unapology. After she died,
a man tried to erase all evidence she existed. When they
found her sarcophagus in 1903, it was empty.

The first time I confessed to having a crush
on a girl was in my journal. Hieroglyphics
barely legible, a language I refused to speak:
   There is a girl
I didn't dare call it what it was, couldn't

bring myself to say *lesbian*. I buried it in my childhood
bedroom—pink and so *typical*—in the boys I'd liked
at a distance. They found Hatshepsut in an anonymous
tomb, the body identified by a missing tooth,
her mouth claiming herself

even in death. Now I use my mouth to kiss my wife.
To say *Lesbian Lesbian Lesbian* to strangers, in
classrooms, in poems, at my family's dinner table,
my body my own temple of unapology, unburied
and unwilling to be silenced.

GSA

One girl lies and tells her mom she's in a Culture Club.
One girl tells us about both times she came out,

the first time, as a gay boy. One student gives us a new
name and pronoun to call them, but *only at club meetings.*

One made rainbow cupcakes for a bake sale before
her parents banned her from attending. One boy

wears nail polish and eyeliner and reads us his poetry
about boys and manatees. One student gifts us with

a lesson on Black activists, on how intersectionality
means no one gets left out. One girl wears a suit

to prom. One boy hovers at the doorway. One girl
wears a gay themed shirt everyday—her favorite says

No One Knows I'm a Lesbian. One girl puts up club flyers
even if they get torn down. One boy keeps reminding

us that a Pride Day at school is a bad idea, that people
will say things. *I'm just being realistic.* But they put on their

rainbow attire anyway. I watch them roam the halls
from my classroom doorway — marquees of color

splashed among the crowd. The day a student asked me
in the middle of class if I was gay I said yes, even

though a teacher at a nearby school was fired for being
a bride with another bride, even though later,

a conservative radio station would post my engagement
photo online like a Wanted poster. Who better

to prepare me, to teach me how to live life outside
of a closet than the same kids who clap every time I say

my wife? Who gather around her picture on my desk
like it's a holy grail, who are so desperate for heroes,

they wear pride flags tied around their necks as capes,
become the heroes themselves.

What if Our Love Wasn't

a movement. If holding hands in public
was not the bravest thing I did today.
If introducing you as my wife was not
an act of revolution met with equal parts
applause and sneers, if Orlando
was another random shooting,
not bigotry that bloodied the night.
If our wedding was just another
wedding, not pictures captioned
love wins. And the election was just
an election. A morning
I didn't even check the news,
just kissed you goodbye as you
slept, careful not to wake you
from a world still soft enough
to dream.

Lesbian Fashion Struggles

Formalwear is toughest—
so suit or dress, so senior prom,
binary bursting

from every corsage
and boutonniere.
The day before a wedding

my wife and I tear through
our closets, model outfits
for each other in hopes

we'll find something
that doesn't feel like a costume,
but like our own skin.

We try on words: *butch,*
femme, androgynous.
But language always fails.

The children we won't birth
line up on the shelf like shoes,
the men we won't love

hang limp
on their hangers
in the back.

Still, our closets are filled
of sleeves empty with possibility,
extended toward us.

Ode to Flannel

You rainbow of plaid
lined up in my closet.
The only good part
of winter. I love you
in classic lumberjack
red, like the old shirt
my grandfather gave me.
A slight mothball smell,
buttons on a different side
than I'm used to, fastened
all the way up.
Sleeves rolled mid-
way—ready to chop
some wood,
or shotgun
a beer, or hold
a woman close
by a campfire.
I also love you
tied around my waist
like a skirt, or flag
I wave, a splash of texture
with my dark lipstick,
all those lines inter-
woven like fingers
laced together under
tables. You queen
of the layer. Sometimes
a light jacket. Un-
buttoned. The perfect
transition piece
when the first leaf turns
gold. You were the only
cliché I could claim,
hanging in my closet
long before I came out

of it. Before I even knew
any of the stereotypes—
only that I didn't
fit them.

Sometimes I Feel Sorry for the Clothes I Buy

but never wear, the ones I double back for and pluck
from the rack on impulse, that I smuggle into dressing
rooms in my search for something that looks like

anyone but me, or who I could be if I was braver
with fewer fucks to give. The ones I take home
to never leave my bedroom, Rapunzels in my tower.

The blazer with the tag hanging from its sleeve
like a garter that should long be ripped off,
the one that turns my black pants into a suit if only

I'd let it. The blue tube of lipstick that touches
my lips when no one else is around, my secret
girl, my bruised lady of the night. The loudmouth

jumpsuit tight enough to tell every curve, backless
except for strips like guitar strings begging
for someone to strum them. The black top

that shows a whisper of stomach with slits
in the sleeves. The men's button-down I fasten
all the way up, too snug on my hips, my body

too woman in its embrace. These clothes deserve
to know the heat of a body, to be worn
out, not just used for practice as I finger

their fabric. They lie on my bed like French girls
saying, *Don't paint me unless you are going to take me
to dinner or a movie or dancing or hell, even a drive.*

*Don't take your picture with me if you're just going
to delete it before anyone sees. I dare you:
Be this woman you pretend to be.*

The Only Girl Out at My High School

wore a lot of black. Her pants
were wide and bedazzled

with chains. She had a lip ring.
Wore a rainbow of bracelets

stacked to her elbow. I remember her
walking down the hall with two girls,

and I wondered if one was her love.
I wondered if it was lonely, being a stereo

of pride, bass booming, intimidating
and loud and all of the things girls weren't

supposed to be in that small Arkansas town
where kids debated over religion between classes,

said women were supposed to be silent
and gay people were going to hell.

My parents told me to take a walk,
not a stand, and I mostly listened.

Slow danced at prom
with my own shadow. My face,

a bouquet of scarlet anytime
my name was called in class.

I was a violin with the strings
plucked out, a symphony

of silence, exactly who
I was taught to be.

She was her own marching
band, parading down the halls

and even the religious ones
respected her. Liked her taste

in music. I once sat with her
on an empty stage after play practice

and watched her go through a playlist
on her laptop. I don't remember

the songs, but I remember we laughed.
I remember the way I felt

awkward, but also excited. How I paid
attention. Like I was hearing an overture,

collecting the melodies
so someday

I could sing them.

Ode to the Word Lesbian

They say you take up too much space in the mouth,
all those awkward syllables fighting to be
pronounced—the heavy L, the way the tongue must
        meet teeth to birth you.

        I once took you out of a slide about
        Audre Lorde because my students' laughter
        at your mention was so disruptive: *Black, lesbian,*
        mother, warrior, poet. I recited her quote about
        silence, the one that ends
                it's better to speak, and ignored

the irony of my censorship. *Lesbian,* often rejected
for sounding clinical, your sound more like a diagnosis
or medication with a slew of undesirable side effects—
in 1925, you were a noun that meant the female
        equivalent of a sodomite, an *inversion.*

        When I was 13 and growth-spurted above my
        classmates, a well-meaning man came up to us
        in the grocery store and told my father, *Someday*
        a tall man is going to come and take her away from
        you. How could he ever
                have imagined you?

The third section of your definition reads: *erotic;*
sensual, as if you are x-rated, a word that must
be whispered, much too shameful to be said
in broad daylight, porn shoved
        under the mattress.

        In high school, a boy told me the locker room
        was littered with rumors that I was a lesbian.

The baseball team decided it was *hot*, okay
as long as you looked like a boy could still insert
            himself in the fantasy.

I have to mention your mother-
land, Lesbos, surrounded by salt-slick
water with Sappho and her anguished
love poems and don't we all live
there, or wish we did? An island
of women who wear crowns of mouths
that don't know how to quiet, who damn
the uncomfortable, who owe men nothing,
            who own their desire.

Doing My Mother's Makeup

I try my new lipstick on her. Its fire
engine red sirens across her lips.
They look fuller, almost pouty.
Well I need the face to go
with it. She gets comfortable
in her chair. Closes her eyes
and leans into it. *I can't believe*
you're making me do this, she teases,
though it was her idea. I can feel the lonely

as I dab on concealer, shadow
her eyelids, finding parts of me in her
face. The green eyes. The sparse
brows. Tonight is Christmas Eve,
and she will ask my father to pray over
the meal even though they haven't
been married for years, even though

we never pray, her wifely duties
a phantom itch that resurfaces
in his presence, like the years I played
my part—kissed men who wanted me
with no thought of if I wanted
them. This year is the first time
I've brought someone home.

My future wife sits in the living room.
You both just look so normal, my mom
had once said. *Which one of you*
cooks? Who pays when you go out?
I'd tried to explain a world without
such rules. But how to explain
this unlearning? When I'm done

with her makeup, she disappears
into her closet. Returns with earrings

to complete the look. Admires,
for a moment, her reflection. *I bet
no one will notice*, she says, then
walks back out to the kitchen to finish
making dinner.

Halloween is the Queer Christmas

We decorate ourselves instead of a tree.
Put lights behind pumpkins' twinkling smiles,
the garland and bows on us, not a mantle. Our Santa
is Marsha P. Johnson or Laverne Cox or Lena Waithe

or Freddie Mercury or anyone who gave us the gift
of their bold, donned a stage in their gay apparel
and gave us permission to do the same.
No awkward family dinners performing *normalcy*—

just candy and a chance to be
someone else, or more ourselves,
the truth called costume
for the night.

We sing our carols at the altar
of a karaoke machine: RENT and Cher,
rounds of *Time Warp* and *Monster Mash*, a choir
of skeletons and ghosts and zombies,

all so very alive.
Tis the season to be
proud, to trade our silent nights
for this holy loud.

Lesbian Shoes

In college, my gay friend called my shoes
Lesbian shoes. They were Birkenstock
knock offs, worn fake leather sandals.
Anytime I wore them, or anything
he deemed unfashionable: *Lesbian.*

One Friday night, he declared that maybe
I was a lesbian. Everyone laughed at this idea
as ridiculous as their boyfriends wearing
stilettos. My roommate once called me
Obviously Pretty, meaning too blonde, too

cheerleader, too Cinderella not to decorate
a man's arm, to hope he chases after me
at midnight. Me, a *lesbian*? Even more
far-fetched than any fairytale I grew
up reading, than any dream I dared

to dream. I played along, joked that maybe
this explained my questionable fashion
choices, why every time I found myself
in a man's arms, I wanted to crawl out
of my skin. And maybe his queerness

saw my queerness, maybe it was a truth
I could only face dressed in alcohol and laughter,
disguised as a joke, the glass slipper I tried on
in the glitter of night and took back
off again when morning came.

All the Closeted Characters from My Childhood March in a Pride Parade

Scout skates with her roller-derby team. Tattooed
arms burst out of her *Dyke* tank top, her knees bruised
like summers blustering through Maycomb. Dumbledore

hands out flyers that say *Transgender women*
are women, smiles over his half-moon spectacles.
Mercutio walks on stilts in a crop top

and wings, makeup flawless, a tattoo with the initials
RM barely visible above his heart. Mulan holds a sign
that says *Non-Binary is Beautiful*, their hair shaved

on the sides. Nancy Drew drives her blue convertible,
"Come to My Window" turned all the way up. I sing along
and wave—they are the crew I always wanted.

Here, I am the child I could have been. Some days
are hard—friends avoid me, my parents' flustered
confusion. But there is also beauty:

My first kiss with a girl at summer camp, our lips
two sparks in the night, instead of with the boy
who silenced my mouth with his. My first

heartbreak, driving by my ex's cry-singing
Tegan and Sara, instead of the hollow ache,
my heart a match no man could light.

My wife is not the first woman
I will let myself love. I am still bruised
but in different ways. Here the world is filled

with possibilities. Here I see them, am waving as they
pass, mirrors creating a kaleidoscope
of reflections until I can see
myself.

Self-Portrait as a Hayley Kiyoko Music Video

After Danez Smith

I wear Hawaiian shirts. Not ironically. Not dad-
on-vacation style, but Lesbian Jesus style—impossibly
suave, the V of the unbuttoned fabric framing
my sports bra, hibiscus flowers rippling in the breeze.

It's California, so the weather is always sunset
lighting, perfect for bomber jackets and slight
head nods to girls across the room, whole
conversations shared in the longing of a stare.

Girls are always meeting in bathrooms, not to fix
makeup or gossip, but to lick the salt off
each other's necks, mouth desire there
like secrets that break against the shore
of skin again and again.

A swagger of women dance. They conjure
the swoon from each other's hips with just a smirk,
know how to touch a woman but make her wait
for it, tease the air between them until she's dizzy

with wanting. There is always a pool table,
perfect for dancing against with a girl
I never kissed but wanted
to. Here, I don't even wait for the closet
of a bathroom. Here, I kiss her in the living
room, right there in the open
where everyone can see.

My Grandmother Gives Me Her Approval Nine Years After Her Death

After my grandfather died, we walked through
the house-turned-museum of my grandparents' life

together, relics from every drawer and closet pulled out
for inspection. My dad called me into the dining room,
pointed at the gold-rimmed plates displayed in the glass

cabinet next to what was left of their wedding china.
The plates had scenes of Victorian women draped

across furniture and each other painted in the middle,
little cherubs surrounding them with harps.
Your aunt looked these up. They're called Lesbian Plates,

my dad said in a hushed voice. *I'm sure your grandmother
had no idea what she was buying when she got these,*

*but we thought
you may want them.*

On the Drive Home from the Transgender Day of Visibility Celebration, We Pull over

A bird screams
in the empty

parking lot.
My wife tells me

she's a killdeer,
birds that have

had to adapt
to civilization,

their ground nests
in places like this—

the smallest scrap
of green in a sea

of asphalt.
They are not

predatory,
toothpick legs

and beaks
all so breakable.

They protect
their nests

by pretending
to have a broken

wing, their screams
a siren that lures

danger away.
After I'd pulled

my wife away
from the men

throwing punches
on the state capitol

steps, we circled
the podium,

the smallest island
of queers, the air

around us heavy
with hate, red

hats puncturing
the sky. Our leader

told us *Don't
engage,* said

*Look inward,
at each other.*

So we fought
back tears

and sang,
got louder when

one of us broke
down and could

not speak. I held
my love's hand

like a lifeboat.
I could pass

as these men's
sisters or wives,

but here I am
so visible.

So many
in our circle

have no choice
but to be seen,

every walk
down the street

filled with
potential

predators.
My wife just

came out at work
as non-binary

last week.
With her

short hair
and boyish

clothes, she
looks like

so much
of what these

men hate,
and I want

so badly to
protect her.

In the empty
parking lot,

this bird
keeps

screaming.
I wonder

what danger
she sees.

Communion

My girlfriend got an invite from her college RA (who'd
fallen in love with her prayer partner at the all-girls
bible study). It was a fundraiser these lesbians had been
running for over a decade, an underground event
that changed locations every year to keep it as safe
as possible. When we pulled up, there were no signs.
Just a dark building that looked almost abandoned.
When we opened the door, our eyes were filled

with a cathedral of light. Life. Button-down shirts
and gray-haired women. Short-haired women. Stage
performers making their offerings—lip syncing
to Shania Twain's "Man! I Feel Like a Woman!", sequin
dresses shimmying, suits two-stepping, hair slicked back
and thumbs looped around suspenders as they mouthed
the words *I want to be free yeah, to feel the way I feel.*
A silent auction where women walked down aisles
and perused the items, holding hands.

I'd never been around so many lesbians in my life.
We sat back and watched the communion of it all.
Where did they come from? I asked, wondering why
when we walk down the street it always feels
like we are the only lesbians in Arkansas *They keep
to themselves. This is how they lived when they were our age,*
my girlfriend said, *in secret.*

We sat on fold-out chairs more comfortable than any
church pew and pondered over their ties and mullets,
their dance moves, over which kind we'd grow up
to be. For a moment we forgot the price of visibility.
There was no preacher or pulpit, no mention of God,
but I could hear the Amens, could feel the holy

ghosts of those who came before us. Drunk off joy,
we strutted our way to the dance floor where we held
each other, giddy and grinning at the couple next to us,
women who laughed and kissed, then looked our way and pointed,
urging us to do the same.

Sex Education

There's a story that always makes my father
laugh, that he says defines my personality:
I'm six, my sister is eight. There are two dogs
in our front yard. *Aww look, they're in love*, I say.
My sister corrects me. *No they're not—*
they're just having sex. It hadn't occurred to me
there was a difference.

My mother fumbles as she tries
to talk to me about sex. I have questions—
about masturbation, pregnancy, the blood
in my underwear. She sighs and says, finally,
Honestly, it's not that great.

In health class, we are separated by gender.
Shy, we look at pictures of the reproductive organs.
This is a penis. This is a vagina. The penis
goes here. This is sex. When I hear rumors
that two girls were found kissing
in the locker room, their basketball coaches smirk
and say girls sometimes *experiment*.

We have borrowed each other's bodies
for years. He calls, I stumble
out of the bar and into his bed.
The first time I said *no*, he coaxed
my body open, a closed bud
he pushed to bloom between
his fingers. I cannot do this sober
without crying. He cannot comfort or make me
come. Once, I woke up in his arms
and my own urine. Once, he told me
he loved me—another accident
spilled across his bed.

I dream of kissing her long before
we ever do. In my dream we take turns
pushing each other against a wall, pressing
hard. We match. The reality is a cold day.
She walks me to my car before asking if she could.
My *yes*. My *please do*. Hard. Urgent. Much better
than *great*, no experiment or accident—
her mouth, the summer
I've been waiting for my whole gray life.

A Toast

Today we drink champagne
for breakfast, straight

from the bottle. Fry eggs
and use the spatula

as a microphone.
Dance when the song

demands to be danced to.
You kiss me between

laughter and we overcook
the eggs.

This week I picked a dress
for our wedding

and one for a funeral.

I know it should feel wrong,
to dance, but nothing

feels more necessary than to take
another slice of champagne, spin you

around and pull you in close, bury
my face in your hair.

Let the toast
burn.

Pilgrimage

My hands
  have never
looked as beautiful
  as when
they are on you.
Your back
  is a canvas,
a Pollock,
  a freckled
Starry Night.
  Even in the midst
of a masterpiece
  my hands know
what to do.
  Weary travelers
thankful
  for the journey
here.
  To see this.
All those stars.
  It took
light years
  to get here.

ACKNOWLEDGMENTS

Thank you to the editors of the following journals who first published these poems, sometimes in earlier forms:

NAILED: "Hatshepsut," "Granddaddy's Closet," "Ode to Flannel," "Doing My Mother's Makeup," "Self—Portrait as a Hayley Kiyoko Music Video"

Glass: A Journal of Poetry: "A Toast"

Barrelhouse: "Sometimes I Feel Sorry for the Clothes I Buy," "My Grandmother Gives Me Her Approval Nine Years After Her Death," "All the Closeted Characters From My Childhood March in a Pride Parade"

Brave Voices: "The Only Girl Out At My High School"

Thimble: "Lesbian Shoes"

SWWIM Every Day: "Lesbian Fashion Struggles"

Nimrod International Journal: "Lipstick," "What If Our Love Wasn't"

Stonewall Fifty: "GSA"

Bible Belt Queers: "Where I Come From"

Prong & Posy: "Blonde"

Endless gratitude to my teachers and mentors at Queens University, particularly Rebecca Lindenberg, Ada Limón, and Cathy Smith Bowers. You all taught me so much not just about being a better writer, but about being a better teacher of writing.

Also thanks to the writer friends who I had the privilege to continue sharing poetry and feedback with while working on this manuscript, most notably Laurel Page, Katy Mullins, and Amanda Gomez.

Thanks and love to my friend Karen Hayes, who I wrote most of this book across from at Guillermo's Gourmet Coffee. Your legacy of service and love and joy in our little writing community is one that will always live on. We miss you. I still want to be you when I grow up.

I owe so much to Megan Falley and her online class—she was the first to comb through this chapbook with me as it started to take shape. Thank you for believing in me. Thank you for being such a badass femme and mentor.

Thanks to Erin Smith and the Sundress Academy for the Arts for my residency on Firefly Farm—my week there was short, but filled with writing and community and love.

Thank you to Seth Pennington and Bryan Borland for giving this manuscript a home, and for being such a beacon of hope in Arkansas and beyond for the LGBTQ community.

Thank you to my family—my mom, my dad, my sisters Lizzie and Mary, and my brother Thomas—for your support and love. My story could have been so different, and I'm so thankful for the way you not only accept me, but celebrate me.

To my wife, Bonnie—thank you for being so many of these poems' first reader and cheerleader. I am so grateful for you, and for our love story. Here's to all the haircuts and outfits we have yet to try, to the thousand different ways we'll continue to grow.

THE POET

Caroline Earleywine teaches high school English in Central Arkansas where she tries to convince teenagers that poetry is actually cool. She has her MFA from Queens University in Charlotte and lives in Little Rock with her wife and two dogs.

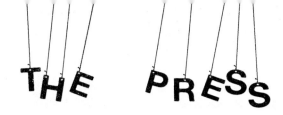

THE PRESS

Sibling Rivalry Press is an independent press based in Little Rock, Arkansas. It is a sponsored project of Fractured Atlas, a nonprofit arts service organization. Contributions to support the operations of Sibling Rivalry Press are tax-deductible to the extent permitted by law, and your donations will directly assist in the publication of work that disturbs and enraptures. To contribute to the publication of more books like this one, please visit our website and click *donate*.

Sibling Rivalry Press gratefully acknowledges the following donors, without whom this book would not be possible:

Anonymous (18)
Arkansas Arts Council
John Bateman
W. Stephen Breedlove
Dustin Brookshire
Sarah Browning
Billy Butler
Asher Carter
Don Cellini
Nicole Connolly
Jim Cory
Risa Denenberg
John Gaudin
In Memory of Karen Hayes
Gustavo Hernandez
Amy Holman
Jessica Jacobs & Nickole Brown
Paige James
Nahal Suzanne Jamir
Allison Joseph
Collin Kelley
Trevor Ketner

Andrea Lawlor
Anthony Lioi
Ed Madden & Bert Easter
Mitchell, Blackstock, Ivers & Sneddon, PLLC
Stephen Mitchell
National Endowment for the Arts
Stacy Pendergrast
Simon Randall
Paul Romero
Randi M. Romo
Carol Rosenfeld
Joseph Ross
In Memory of Bill Rous
Matthew Siegel
Alana Smoot
Katherine Sullivan
Tony Taylor
Leslie Taylor
Hugh Tipping
Guy Traiber
Mark Ward
Robert Wright

CPSIA information can be obtained
at www.ICGtesting.com
Printed in the USA
JSRBC011709090920
7674JS00002BB/188